CIE Buses
in colour photographs by John Sinclair
John Sinclair

Thirty coaches (P161-70/271-90) had the same body shell with a full front and an ornamental radiator grille with the CIE emblem in gold. With a one piece opening door, 30 coach seats, internal luggage racks, a public address system and heaters they entered service on tours in the current coach livery of light green with a dark green flash. In 1955, they were repainted into the primrose yellow and grey coach livery of the U class and used for local sightseeing. The last ten retained these colours until withdrawn. P289, built in 1951, heads a line-up of stored coaches at Albert Quay Depot in Cork. It became a school bus at Sligo in 1967, was delicensed in 1970 and scrapped at Inchicore in 1973.

Introduction

Having reached the age of 16 living in a family with no car, I decided to try my hand at hitch-hiking in order to visit bus companies distant from my home in Edinburgh. Inspired by the frontispiece of *Buses Illustrated* No. 1 titled "The last tram to Dalkey," a friend and I set out in April 1958 to hitch around Ireland which we managed with great ease, although we had to stow away in a cargo boat to return to Scotland, having run out of money. Fascinated by the characterful buses, I returned the following year and cycled in Counties Mayo, Kerry and Cork, the most vivid memories being of Leyland TD5s R185-6 at Salthill where I stayed in Galway.

Having acquired a 35mm camera in 1961, and photographed around Scotland, I returned in 1964 to take colour slides, and spent three weeks hitch-hiking around Ireland, the most memorable lift being from the political historian, the late Conor Cruise O'Brien, who transported me for three days. This book was written principally to show the pictures from this visit. However, it also includes a selection of single deckers new to CIE or the GNR between 1947 and 1974 when the last of the M class entered service, a date which defined the end of construction of bus bodies at CIE's Spa Road Works in Dublin.

There are already excellent illustrated books written on Irish bus operators, from which I have obtained further information to supplement my own which is derived from copious notes, lists and timetables. In particular the magnum opuses of Cyril McIntyre's *CIE Buses* and Sam Simpson's *Great Northern Railway of Ireland Road Motor Services* are authoritative works. This book is intended simply to show a representative selection of colour pictures of some of the buses featured in these books. Hopefully, they characterise a colourful era in Irish transport history, which has now inevitably gone for ever.

© John Sinclair, 2016
First published in the United Kingdom, 2016,
by Stenlake Publishing Ltd.
www.stenlake.co.uk
ISBN 9781840337464

Printed by:
Berforts, 17 Burgess Road, Hastings, TN35 4NR

The M class of 213 12 metre Leyland Leopard PSU5 was the last to be built at Spa Road, using frames supplied by Metal Sections of Oldbury. M1-30 entered service in 1971 with 48 seats in the brown and cream coach livery for express services. M13 seen here on Achill Island in 1985, was later repainted into the 1975 Expressway livery which it unusually retained until withdrawn in 1998, and nearby school bus MDS2 also retained this livery until withdrawn in 2000. When the M class was becoming surplus, it was one of the earliest to become a school bus in 1986, perhaps because it was not re-engined. One of three buses outstationed at Dooagh for services to Westport, it was photographed in 1985 near Dooninver on the 10.45 departure from Dooagh.

Donegal was the last area of operation for the Gardners acquired with the bus operation of Great Northern Railways in October 1958. Now all out of use, and parked up at Donegal Depot in 1964 are some of the last batch (G385-402) which were 33 seat dual purpose vehicles with Clayton bulkhead heating and interior luggage racks, constructed using Park Royal body frames completed at the GNR body shop at Dundalk. G398 is in standard CIE livery, while 399, originally in the reverse "Dundalk" version, was repainted into coach colours to provide additional vehicles for the 1960 and 1961 tour seasons, continuing in service until August 1963. Just in view is P318 returned from the CDR for transfer to Ballina, one of eleven PS2/14 hired in June for its summer operation in Donegal, which ended up as a towcar at Sligo Depot.

Only school buses and double deckers were built at Spa Road between 1954 and 1961 when a new service bus, the last to be designed and built by CIE, appeared. The E class of 170 Leyland Leopards were fitted with 45 high backed seats with divided rests and a jack-knife folding door at the front which was power operated for OMO operation which was being introduced on provincial services from 1961. There was a capacious rear locker, a rear reversing light and a rear destination screen as seen in E130, recently into service and allocated to Sligo Depot, which has just arrived in Donegal from Ballyshannon. Operating in the north west all its life, it was never classified as a school bus, and was sanctioned for scrapping at Stranorlar Depot in June 1985.

Their OMO status was shown by a sign displaying "pay as you enter" below the nearside windscreen as seen on E106 photographed near Kinvara Youth Hostel on the 9.00 service from Lisdoonvarna to Galway. It also has the twin headlights fitted to the later order of 80 vehicles. The E class were the last CIE vehicles to be delivered with traditional roof-mounted luggage carriers, and the first to have interior luggage racks and floor heaters. They also had a public address system, and were ideally suited to the challenging Irish roads. E106 remained allocated to Galway, becoming a school bus in 1975 and ending up as a driver trainer at Cork until 1996.

Donegal was also the last area in which these rugged vehicles operated. Apart from E151 which had come to Waterford from Ballina in 1982 being relicensed for non OMO service work during the summer of 1984, only eight remained active in the north west. These included E119 and E154 which were photographed at Letterkenny Bus Station in August of that year. E154 had been among the final batch of vehicles to be hired by the CDR when it ceased operation in 1971. In the background are three of the class, formerly E160, 131 and 127, sold to Lough Swilly and now awaiting scrap. E119 was delicensed in July 1985, and 154 earlier that year both buses ended up as a source of spare parts for Lough Swilly. By then only E152 remained in service, at Ballyshannon over the summer, and finally as a school bus at Pettigo.

The next intake of Leopards during 1965-8 were 9.1 metre (C1-190) and 11 metre (C191-270) chassis showcasing the last body to be exclusively designed by CIE. Of all-metal construction, they were assembled at Spa Road from frames supplied by Metal Sections of Oldbury. C71-99 were allocated to Donnybrook Depot for Dublin city services, but in 1966 C71-9 were repainted into coach livery and reseated for the airport service, and transferred to Summerhill Depot. Later C74, now in "desert sand" tan livery with 45 bus seats was reallocated to Donnybrook and was last used on a crew operated shift on the 44B service from the mountain village of Glencullen, before transfer to Stranorlar Depot in 1984. It was photographed in Ballybofey on service from Killybegs to Strabane in June 1985. Two months later it was scrapped.

The last surviving member of the C class was C168 which achieved Bus Eireann livery, and was the only bus kept in Donegal Garage, as seen in this photograph from 1995. It had a regular driver with school runs which included providing a duplicate from Mountcharles to Donegal Secondary School, but was available for service work. Entering service in April 1966, it was transferred from Galway, its home depot from new, to Stranorlar in 1985 joining C163 and 166 in the schools fleet which were painted in yellow schoolbus colours and withdrawn in 1995. C168, however, continued until 1998 completing 32 years in service, being off licence by the time I saw it in June of that year.

C201-20 and 261-70 entered service in this distinctive coach livery of brown and cream with 48 seats as they were immediately required for tours. C253-60 also appeared in these colours with 45 seats for express work. With power-assisted steering, semi-automatic transmission and air suspension, they were well-equipped for a variety of roles. Galway Depot had a long history of retaining the coach livery on older vehicles which were superbly presented, and C270, photographed at the depot in 1985 was still regularly used on day tours such as the Cliffs of Moher. By 1986 all of the C class had become school buses and C270 was moved to Ballina as a school bus, but was also used at Westport on the Louisburgh service. Later it was employed on schools based at the seaside village of Killala, and was withdrawn still in its original livery in October 1989.

C234 however had entered service as a 53 seat service bus at Broadstone Depot in 1966, but two years later it was one of five (231-5) repainted into express livery and reseated with 45 coach seats, similar to C253-60. It was reallocated to Galway for a new seasonal service to Belfast, and remained at that depot until withdrawn, later sharing duties on the local popular tours with C270. Photographed in 1994, it had been repainted from coach colours into yellow and white school bus livery in 1986 and reclassified CS, later undergoing a body overhaul in 1992. Operating in this role, initially based at Abbeyknockmoy and subsequently Athenry, it was withdrawn in January 1995, and passed in to preservation.

The most memorable coaches retained at Galway were two Leyland Worldmasters, WVH13 and 22, new in 1964 and rebodied by Van Hool in 1970 and 1971 respectively. In June 1985 they were used to inaugurate a Galway to Glasgow weekend express service, and repainted into a striking coach livery they were photographed at Galway Depot in July. Also still used for relief work on the London service, for which they were refurbished in 1975, they now seated 49 passengers in upgraded seats and were fitted with curtains, a radio and a microphone. This livery affords a comparison with the KE class Bombardier in the background, new in 1981 in CIE Tours livery without a destination box.

WVH22 was repainted again into current express livery by 1988 and both subsequently into the later version as seen when they were parked up delicensed at the back of Galway Depot in 1997, still officially in the promotional fleet. The official withdrawal dates were July 1996 for WVH22 and November 1996 for WVH13, already 32 years old and now preserved. They had been used on local day tours such as round Connemara, and also routinely on expressway work, particularly weekend helps. WVH 13 was still being used at Longford on such duties when I visited in April 1996 and WVH22 had recently visited both Dublin and Waterford.

The original red and traffic yellow expressway livery introduced in 1975 is exemplified by MG176 seen here at Busáras in 1984 on the Letterkenny express, a service it operated from new in 1972. M170-193 had been used on express services in brown and cream colours, but 176 was still allocated to this service in 1985. Bombardier KE11 had been officially rostered when new in 1981 but proved unreliable and once again MG176 became the preferred vehicle. With curtains and high-backed seats it was still immaculate, but had been downgraded to a service bus by 1990, was officially classified as a school bus in 1995, and withdrawn by April 1996 when it was parked up at Stranorlar Depot, by then in a simplified version of the current expressway livery.

The liveries of the M class were a bewildering assortment over 30 years as they were downgraded from their original roles, and their bodies were modified and reseated. MD127 however, seen here at Ballina Bus Station, was one of the original batch of 55 seat service buses to arrive there new. The depot engineer told me that he volunteered to accept a full allocation of these 12 metre vehicles to prove they were safe on narrow, tortuous Irish roads. In the current expressway livery, it is returning from Sligo to its regular outbase at Ballycastle in 1991. It was repainted into bus livery in 1994, reseated in 1995, and although not classified on paper as MDS, it was latterly used as a school bus, being one of the final seven of the M class to be withdrawn in July 2001.

The last batch of the M class (M194-213) also entered service in coach colours with 48 seats intended for CIE tours, but the demand had lessened due to political problems, and within two years they were used on express services. As such they were not fitted with destination boxes, and M203 seen here in Westport in 1985 departing for Dooagh, displays the usual prominent, informative boards, a common practice for buses based at Ballina. It is already in basic service bus livery, and was demoted to school work in 1989 based for many years at Crossmolina near the northern shores of Lough Conn. All of the M class were officially classed as school buses by 1997 and it was taken out of service in 1999, but still parked up at Ballina in 2001.

Like Galway Depot, Tralee also tended to operate its express service vehicles in coach colours longer than other depots, and MD72 seen at the adjacent bus station was new as a service bus in 1971. However, thirteen years later it is in brown and cream colours, about to depart on the 3.30 service to Dingle which continues to Dunquin Head. One of two buses outstationed at Dingle, it was declared a school bus in November 1992 and withdrawn in 1999. By contrast, MG77 from the same batch but now in expressway livery is on the scenic summer service from Cork to Galway via Lisdoonvarna. It too became a school bus in 1994 being withdrawn in 1999.

Also from Tralee Depot and in traditional coach livery is MD193, the last of the later batch for expressway services. Parked at Killarney in 1985, it has arrived on the summer service from Shannon Airport via Limerick. Classified as MD, it is one of 72 from the M class re-engined with DAF power units due to unsatisfactory performance from the original Leyland engines. A further 81 (MG) received General Motors engines with Allison transmission, and two Cummins units, of which one (MC167) was retained. Some of the original Leyland engines were then fitted to the relatively underpowered 53 seat service buses of the C class. Although fitted with a destination aperture, it inevitably required an additional board for the intermediate stops on the complex expressway network. Downgraded to school work in September 1990, it too was withdrawn in 1999.

The most luxurious M allocated to Tralee at that time was MD200, available for tours but also used on the Limerick service along with the identical MG213, similarly fitted with curtains, an internal destination display and 53 upgraded seats, but in traditional expressway livery. It has an elegant local interpretation of the coach livery featuring "coach tours." However, even its fate was to become a school bus as early as 1991, and again it was withdrawn in 1999. Interestingly, similar MD208 at Stranorlar, which was destroyed by fire in February 2000, retained its original coach colours to the end. Truly no two buses in the M class were absolutely identical at the end of their lives.

Also looking immaculate in the Tralee variant of the coach livery as seen in 1985 is Leyland Royal Tiger Worldmaster WVH19, Tralee's dedicated coach used for the Ring of Kerry circular tour. New in 1964 as WT21, its Van Hool Vistadome replacement body was fitted in 1970. Seating 50 in refurbished seats, and with curtains and a PA system it was, however, fitted for OMO operation and used on weekend helps. The previous year it had been in a variant of the traditional brown and cream coach livery. Off tax by June 1987, it was delicensed in September and withdrawn the following year. Tralee's other coach PL34 was outstationed at Kenmare in the summer and Caherciveen in the winter, leaving WVH19 as the front line coach at the parent depot.

While the livery of WVH19 was unique, there were many other variations on the 37 replacement 44 seat Van Hool bodies (for WVH1-23 and LVH34-47) supplied to CIE in 1970-2, and the ten fitted to new Leopard chassis (LVH24-33.) Of these LVH43 was photographed at Killarney in 1985 in the current tours livery displayed by coaches of the Bombardier KE class. It was one of three (LVH41-3) repainted and transferred to Cork for day tours in September 1984 only to be withdrawn two years later. They had previously had a short life at Summerhill Depot on the Dublin Airport service replacing newer PL class Leopards but displaced by Bombardiers KC28-31.

LVH43 was converted from ET10, seen here in Killarney in 1964 not long after entering service. Leopards ET1-13 and Worldmasters WT1-23 were luxurious 40 seat coaches designed by the David Ogle design partnership in Letchworth which entered service between 1962 and 1964. Introducing the cream and brown coach livery, they were the first new coaches since the U class entered service in 1955, but turned out to be the last to be constructed at CIE's Spa Road works. Futuristic in design, they were spectacular in appearance, and provided a commanding view from the high position of the individual seats which were covered in Donegal tweed. Air conditioning was fitted and there was a public address system. Unfortunately they had a short life due to structural faults with their heavy bodies, and were rebodied by Van Hool in 1970-71.

The first batch of underfloor engine coaches in the CIE fleet were the "Banana Boat" U class of Leyland Royal Tigers with PSU1/15 chassis in a new coach livery of primrose yellow and grey. With an appearance influenced by a Southdown Harrington bodied coach previously used on Irish tours, they had a sunshine sliding roof, a centre entrance and individual adjustable armchair seats. U1-20 initially seated 30 and U21-50 had 34 seats, but U45 photographed at Kenmare on tour in 1964, and appropriately named "The Kenmare," later became a 41 seater. Like many of these fine vehicles, it ended up as a school bus, based at Limerick, and was finally scrapped at Letterkenny in March 1973.

U43, photographed at Donegal Diamond, was one of six (U35/9-43) which were later modified to replace the especially designed double deckers introduced on the Dublin Airport service. This was delayed over the introduction of OMO operation, as the conductors employed had health issues which made this service ideal for them. The coaches were painted in the current double decker livery of monastral and cream, and fitted with power-operated centre doors. However, they had a short life in this role being replaced by Leopards C71-9 in 1966. They were then transferred to Cork for the airport service and local services in the area, being withdrawn by 1971.

With the arrival of the "Banana Boats" in 1956, River class coaches P161-70 and P271-80 were converted to 35 seat rear entrance service buses but retaining their coach seats. Destination screens were fitted, as were advertising boards, and the vehicles were used on scheduled service duties. Before the River class entered service, standard P class Tigers were fitted with 30 coach seats and when possible repainted into coach livery, reverting to 39 seat service buses for the winter amd twenty were so treated for the 1949 and 1950 tours season. P275, seen here at the Busáras in 1964, was officially allocated to Broadstone at the time, but was withdrawn later that year, unlike most of the batch which became school buses in 1967.

Also allocated to Broadstone was P279, seen parked at the depot. It later became a school bus at Limerick and was withdrawn in July 1972. On either side, from the final batch of Tigers (P291-361), are P348 just transferred from Sligo and P342. Built in 1953 with luggage carriers, the rear entrance bodies were only 7 feet 6 inches wide for the narrow roads as requested by county councils in the west of Ireland. They were also the first to be fitted with heaters when new. P342 later became a school bus at Athlone and 348 at Ballina surviving until 1971. In the corner, delicensed, is P31, one of the first batch (P31-6 from Cork) to be hired by the CDR in January 1960 when it started operating buses. Departing in October of that year, it returned for the summer in the next three years to supplement a varying fleet of Tigers, some of which were painted in the CDR colours of rose red and a paler cream than CIE. It was withdrawn in 1965.

P151 photographed at the Busáras in 1964, was due to depart on the 12.00 service from Dublin to Limerick, a five hour journey across the country with only a 5 minute stop at Mountrath. Already fifteen years old, and never converted to rear entrance, it had presumably been fitted with heaters by now. With only a year until withdrawal, it had just been transferred from Galway to Limerick, and was deputising for the regular PS2/14 models P358-9, as surprisingly, this service was not yet operated by E class Leopards. It has been painted into the red and cream livery introduced for single deckers in 1960. This was reminiscent of the colours of the Great Southern Railways Company and its predecessor the Irish Omnibus Company which together with the Dublin United Tramways Company amalgamated to form the CIE in 1945.

By comparison, P224 was one of the batch (P216-270) built in 1951 for Dublin city services to replace many of the original DUTC single decks still in regular service, and clearly shares many parts with the R class double deckers. Fitted with roof route number boxes and reverting to a rear entrance with a jack-knife folding door, they had recessed roof luggage carriers, but surprisingly no steps or handrails. Allocated to Donnybrook Depot, it was photographed at Bray Station on staff shuttle duties. Withdrawn in December 1971, it was scrapped at Inchicore Railway Works the following year. Although this batch was the officially designated Dublin single deck city bus of the P class, by 1964 it had been supplemented by others from the provincial fleet, by then converted to rear entrance.

Across the country, the P class represented the quintessential Irish bus of the 1950s, as seen in this picture of P207 taken in 1964 at Parnell Place Bus Station in Cork, which had arrived from Skibbereen, deputising for regular P352 of narrower width. Still retaining its front entrance and original livery, it provides a contrast with the vehicle behind, in the new livery but still showing the "flying snail" CIE emblem, rather than the "broken wheel" replacement introduced that year. New in 1951, it was withdrawn in August 1966 before the school bus scheme came into operation in 1967 when CIE's Tigers were supplemented by 50 acquired from Ulsterbus. Those were all withdrawn by the end of 1969, but fifteen of CIE's own Tigers were still on school transport

The Royal Tiger service buses (U51-88) were built at Spa Road in 1954, and U71-88 were effectively an underfloor version of P216-70. Only 7 feet 6 inches wide, they were rear entrance with 45 seats, had route number indicators and roof luggage carriers, but no ladders. Initially used on Dublin city services, once the C class arrived and the busy 45 route to Bray had been converted to double deck operation, they were reallocated to provincial depots and fitted with roof ladders. U77 was photographed in Cork in 1964 on Kinsale Road, heading for the seaside resort village of Ballycotton. Two years later, it was converted to dual door for OMO operation in Dublin with 41 seats, later reduced to 39 to accommodate space for a pram, although the centre exit was never used. It was withdrawn in 1971.

By contrast U55 seen at the Busáras, was one of the batch (U51-70) allocated to provincial services when new, and hence has no route number box, but does have steps up to the luggage carrier. Still allocated to Broadstone Depot, it has arrived in from its outstation at Mountmellick. Already converted for OMO operation with a power-operated front door but still with 45 seats, the internal parcel racks have been removed, but its "pay as you enter" sign is not yet in use. It was withdrawn in November 1971 and scrapped at Inchicore Works a year later. Behind it is U65, also allocated to Broadstone which has just arrived from the small agricultural town of of Athboy. Still with its original configuration, it was later rebuilt like U77. By the end of 1965, all of U51-88 were at Dublin city depots and most were dual door. The last to be withdrawn was U79 in 1974.

Unlike CIE, the GNR introduced its first Royal Tiger as early as July 1952, ironically a month before the last Gardner (G402.) entered service U225-8 were the first Leylands to be bought since 1935 and the only ones introduced post-war. Fitted with 44 seat bodies from Saunders-Roe of Beaumaris on Anglesey, they were also only 7 feet 6 inches wide, and with a narrow gangway and being centre door, they were unpopular with customers and staff. When the GNR was taken over in 1958, U225 was at that time allocated to its Dublin Depot, and 226-8 were at Drogheda. In 1964 they were all reallocated (on paper) to Broadstone, and U226, the only one to appear in green livery, has arrived at the Busáras from its regular outstation at Carrickmacross. They were, however, never converted for OMO operation.

In 1965, all four were reallocated to the city depot of Donnybrook to operate the 84 service to the village of Delgany in County Wicklow, and the 44B service to Glencullen. They were the only ex GNR buses to operate on Dublin city services, and all were withdrawn in January 1972 after twenty years in service, U225-6/8 being scrapped at Inchicore in October 1972. However, U227 was still running out of Drogheda Depot in October 1964 when photographed at the bus station. Already, painted into red and cream, it would later have its roof mounted luggage rack removed after transfer to Donnybrook. On the same date, U228 was operating out of Kells outstation into Dublin, and 225 was also based at Carrickmacross, long associated with these vehicles.

After twenty years in service, Leopards E90 and 92 are still on the service allocation at Dundalk Depot, although 91 is outstationed at Monaghan as a school bus in full yellow and cream livery, being the first of the E class to be so classified in August 1974. There was still much variety in the fleet in 1982, and with a period of seven years between the last of the M class entering service and the first of the Bombardier KE class express coaches, and more significantly eleven years before the first Bombardier KR class service bus entered service, older vehicles had to remain in service past their intended date of withdrawal. More significantly, ageing coaches had to be downgraded for local service work. E90 and 92 are approaching the bus station having lost their "pay as you enter" signs but were not withdrawn until 1984.

Parked at Dundalk Bus Station later that morning in April 1982 are 49 seat Leopards PL33 and 36 with Plaxton Panorama Elite bodies from a batch of thirty coaches (PL11-40) bought "off the peg" in 1969 because of an increase in tourist traffic. When this waned again, because of the problems in Northern Ireland, these became surplus and PL11/8-9 and 37/9-40 were sold to Lough Swilly. Now demoted to service work, and converted for OMO operation are PL33 with 54 bus seats and PL36, both being used on short distance routes. PL36 was being scrapped when I visited Dundalk in July 1985, and PL33 was recommended for scrapping in December 1986. PL35 and 38 had been off tax during the winter of 1982, and were also likewise reallocated to Dundalk to replace Leopards of the E class.

The other depot to receive four downgraded Leopard coaches as a stop gap measure was Waterford, which uniquely repainted its cascaded coaches into red bus livery. PL20-2/4 had arrived in 1981 and PL20 was photographed at Clonmel Station in July 1984, converted for OMO operation, with a "pay as you enter" sign and now with 55 bus seats, initially transferred to provide extra capacity for the busy Tramore service. As the regular bus outstationed at Clonmel, it has returned from Waterford at 11.20 and spends the remainder of the day on local and school runs, and being a Friday, it is waiting to depart for the village of Newcastle at 1.20. It was parked up off licence at Waterford Depot the following year, having been replaced by the arrival of KR54.

Waterford Depot also received seven coaches in 1983-84 which had been rebodied by Van Hool in 1970-71. There were four Leopards (LVH37/40/4/6) and three Worldmasters (WVH4/14/21) all remaining as 44 seat coaches, but also repainted into bus livery. WVH14 was photographed at Waterford Bus Station in 1984, at that time sited at the railway station, with the uniquely designed signal box seen in the background. About to leave on a duplicate short working to Mooncoin, it had arrived from Broadstone a year ago, after lying off tax for a while. Originally WT15 (the Worldmasters were not renumbered in sequence) it was withdrawn the following year, and all the Waterford Van Hool coaches were withdrawn by the end of 1987. LVH46 alone had been prepared for a further role as a school bus, but the decision was reversed.

By contrast, all of the Leopard coaches cascaded down to Dundalk Depot at the same time initially retained their coach livery. In addition to the four Plaxton bodied coaches, there were four Leopards rebodied by Van Hool (LVH34-6/9) which were new in 1963-64 with David Ogle designed bodies as ET1-3/6. LVH35 is parked at Dundalk Bus Station in 1984, having arrived from Omeath on the 7.30 am commuter service, and due to depart for Newry at 1.30, later returning to its outbase at Carlingford. Transferred from Broadstone in April 1982, it was initially kept as the spare coach at Monaghan for breakdowns and helps. However, it had been replaced by LVH39 which was a "good starter."

All four Van Hool rebodied Leopards ultimately became school buses at Dundalk, none in schoolbus colours, but acquiring a variety of stripes which approximated to the service bus livery at that time, and were fitted with a variety of bus seats. The first to be reassigned were LVH34 and 36 in 1988, and the last to be withdrawn LVH36 in June 1993 when nearly 30 years old. However, LVH35 had the distinction of being outshopped in full expressway livery, and when photographed at Dundalk Bus Station in 1990 was the regular performer on the Dundalk to Galway express service, with passengers changing buses at Athlone. Reduced to being a school bus in 1992, it was withdrawn at the end of that year.

GNR bought 33 double deckers after the war, of which 31 passed to CIE when the company was acquired in 1958, the last to be withdrawn from the streets of Dublin being in September 1967. All were AEC Regents with bodies constructed using Park Royal frames, but one batch in 1948 (AR433-9) were delivered complete from their works in London, as the GNR body shop at Dundalk was too busy. Of high specification with heaters and interior luggage racks, they seated 56 and were all later fitted with platform doors. AR433 was photographed in Dundalk, displaying the short-lived "reverse" livery whereby the CIE colours had been substituted for the GNR blue and white. One of four allocated to Drogheda at the time of the takeover, it was now operating from Dundalk Depot. New in July 1948, it ran for eighteen years.

AR440-2 were identical Regent 111s, except that their bodies were completed at Dundalk, and they entered service with platform doors in January 1953. Ordered to replace trams on the Hill of Howth tramway system, the closure proved to be temporary, and by June 1958 they were allocated to Dundalk, Carlingford and Drogheda respectively. Northern Ireland only permitted 7 feet 6 inches wide vehicles until the mid 1970s, and these ten AECs were useful for cross border services. AR442 was photographed at Drogheda Bus Station in 1964, also in "Dundalk" livery, and was not scrapped until 1971. Also seen is the rear of AR436 which was new in July 1948, and operated out of Ballyshannon Depot in Donegal in the 1950s. However, it was allocated to the GNR depot at Abercorn Road in Dublin at the time of the takeover, moving to the CIE city depot of Clontarf, but was now back at Drogheda.

The first new double deckers to enter service with CIE after the war were also AECs (AR1-11) but no more followed, and twenty Leyland OPD1 Titans (R261-80) entered service in 1946-47 with eight foot wide, 66 seat bodies, bodies built at Spa Road from the remaining thirteen sets of Leyland parts delivered to the DUTC in 1940 plus seven new bodies in kit form. Half of the batch were fitted with half drop opening windows and half had sliding vents. They had the pre-war 8.6 litre engine and crash gearboxes which were replaced in 1963 with 9.8 litre engines and synchromesh gearboxes from scrapped OPS3 Tigers, and sixteen, including R278 had body overhauls. Classed as a "Queen Mary," it was photographed in Dublin in 1964 in the blue and cream livery introduced in 1961 for double deckers. It was withdrawn in March 1968, the last survivor of a batch allocated to Clontarf Depot for the 30 service to Dollymount.

CIE introduced 573 Leyland PD1 (R261-80) and PD2 (R281-833) models into service between 1946 and 1958, of which 150 (R291-440) were complete vehicles from Leyland buses. R291-390 were of standard chassis and body design with a single line destination display, high standard interior finish and 60 seats. Identical to a large fleet supplied to Bolton Corporation, they were therefore classed as the "Boltons," and allocated to Donnybrook Depot for tram replacement. R391-440 were to Capetown specification with half drop windows, and had standard CIE destination equipment. R412-440 however were only 7 feet 6 inches wide. R400 from Donnybrook Depot was photographed at Bray Terminus, off the 86 route from College Street. New in July 1949 it was withdrawn in 1967, although some "Capetowns" completed 20 years in service.

There was some variety in the vehicles built at Spa Road, and R541-6 entered service on 29th June 1953 taking passengers from the Busáras to Dublin Airport. Initially painted in the green and white Aer Lingus livery with prominent lettering on the side, they were 50 seat coaches with a centre entrance and jack knife doors. There was a large luggage compartment with side and rear doors, and only sixteen passengers in the lower deck, later reduced to fourteen. In 1962, they were repainted into blue and cream, and R544 was photographed at the Busáras in October 1964, shortly before they were replaced by the U class coaches. Remaining at Donnybrook, they were converted to 68 seat service buses with rear entrances subsequently losing their full fronts, with R541/5-6 having theirs removed a year after downgrading to service buses. They were withdrawn in September 1974.

While superficially similar to R278, R575-80 were OPD2/1 special chassis, as they were 7 feet 6 inches wide to accommodate their bodies which came off the six Daimler CWD6 chassis with bodies built at Spa Road in 1946 from parts supplied to the DUTC in 1940 (DR1-6). The only Daimlers operated by CIE, they were withdrawn in 1954-55, their bodies were modified and lengthened by a foot, and the seating capacity increased from 58 to 66. Entering service in 1954 (R575/9-80) or 1955 (R576-8) they continued to operate the same route from Conyngham Road Depot which was the 72 service from Aston Quay to Oxmantown Road, on which R579 (with the body from DR5) was running in 1964. With their seating capacity further increased to 67, they were withdrawn at the end of 1970.

While R565-74 were delivered with platform doors to operate the longer Dublin city services to Maynooth and Enniskerry, others at provincial depots were later fitted with them, notably in 1959 R796 at Sligo Depot which operated up to Ballyshannon. An interesting batch were R678-81, new in 1956, which were especially converted in January 1959 to provide comfortable transport for workers travelling from Cork to the new oil refinery at Whitegate. Pre-war Leyland Titans R4/19/37/140/93-8 had been sent down the previous April to transport the construction workers. R678-81 were fitted with 60 coach seats, heaters and platform doors, as seen in this picture of R680 at Cork Bus Station in Parnell Place in 1964, which demonstrates the strong Leyland design influence. It still retains its Kakhi roof in a livery inspired by Birmingham City Transport colours, but this was later repainted white. In 1965 it was converted back to 68 bus seats, but retained its platform door, continuing to operate from Cork Depot until withdrawn in 1975.

The final batch of AEC Regents to enter service with the GNR (AR299-307) in 1953 were 66 seat vehicles with platform doors built at Dundalk using Park Royal frames on chassis 30 feet long and 8 feet wide. The high seating capacity was useful for Dublin city services and when acquired by CIE, AR301-4 were thus employed. AR299 was at Dundalk and 306-7 at Drogheda where they remained, 300 and 305 having been destroyed by fire. When GNR's depot at Abercorn Road closed in December 1958, AR301/3-4 moved to the CIE depot at Clontarf where 301 was photographed in 1964. Previously in "reverse" CIE colours, it and 304 achieved the blue and cream livery. While AR301 was withdrawn in April 1967, 304 survived until the autumn, the last of the batch being withdrawn in 1970. Parked beside it is standard OPD2 R515 showing the three piece front upper window. Partly dismantled after withdrawal in November 1973, it was later resurrected to cover a shortage of buses.

Dublin's Donnybrook Depot was arguably the biggest bus depot in Europe in the 1950s, and parked there still in service in 1964 is P21, one of four (P20-1/5-6) of the first batch of 30 OPS3 Tigers still in daily use. With the first CIE bodies designed and built at Spa Road works, similar to those fitted the previous year to the fifteen Leyland TS11 chassis stored since 1940, they were higher than those on P31-361 which followed. Fitted with luggage boots, and also high sided roof luggage carriers shortly after entering service, they were initially used on provincial services. P1-23 were transferred to Dublin city services in 1951 and given route number indicators. Parked beside it is P260 with a rear entrance, from the batch introduced for city services, which became a driver trainer two years later and was scrapped at Inchicore in January 1973.

By contrast, P25 seen in service in red and cream colours, was one of four (P24-7) used on the Dublin Airport service between 1951 and 1953 when they were replaced by R541-6. Fitted with 30 coach seats, they reverted to 39 seat buses for city services, and like P21 had their luggage carriers removed. Surprisingly, however, they were not fitted with route number indicators. P25 has also lost its inadequate rear luggage compartment, giving it an unusual featureless appearance from behind, which contrasts with that of P53 seen inside the front cover of this book. It and P26 were fitted with experimental air suspension, and while P21 and 25 were withdrawn the following year, 26 remained in service until 1971 when at 23 years old it became a towcar at Phibsborough Depot.

While CIE's fleet policy was to order Leylands, GNR favoured AECs, and apart from the four Royal Tigers, it only purchased AECs after the war, possibly because of problems with the sixteen Leyland Lion LT5As purchased in 1934-5. To assist with vehicle replacement, 30 AEC Regal 111 chassis 30 feet long and eight feet wide, with the powerful 9.6 litre engine (A403-32,) were purchased in 1948. First to enter service in June were A427-32 which were timber framed Park Royal bodied 35 seat rear entrance coaches allocated to Drogheda Depot. They were the front line vehicles for hires and tours for six years until the underfloor engine AECs arrived and all ended up as school buses. A432 is seen parked up at Drogheda Depot off licence in 1964. Delicensed in December 1969, it was withdrawn the following year and scrapped at Dundalk in July 1973.

By contrast, A415 photographed in Dundalk shows the features of the service buses (A403-26) which entered service from July with 39 seat bodies completed at the body shop of GNR in Dundalk, with Metal Sections frames supplied by Park Royal. Well appointed internally with heaters and luggage racks, they differed externally, having a split front canopy with the destination screen above the nearside front window, which was unusual for a service bus. They also had sliding vent windows. All of the batch were painted red and cream by January 1964, and they all remained in the Drogheda/Dundalk area until withdrawn. Latterly outstationed at Cootehill, A415 was one of twelve of this batch still in service at Dundalk in 1964, with a further four at Drogheda, and surprisingly A411 allocated to Broadstone and operating out of Cavan. Twelve ended up as school buses in 1967, including A415 which was withdrawn in July 1969.

As CIE was introducing its U class Royal Tigers in 1954, the first of thirty three 7 feet 6 inches wide AEC Regal IVs (AU260-76 and AU331-46) emerged from the GNR body shop at Dundalk. With Park Royal body frames, they had varying seating capacities and differed externally in some respects, but all were rear entrance with a roof luggage carrier and a small rear boot. AU267 was new in May 1955 as a 40 seat service bus allocated to Dublin. The entire batch was converted to front entrance for OMO operation in 1963-64 with 45 seats and air operated doors, displaying a pay as you enter sign. It has also acquired grilles to improve engine cooling. Just transferred from Donegal to Dundalk Depot, it is ready to depart from the Busáras to Edenderry in 1964. Later downgraded to school work, it was withdrawn in May 1972 and scrapped at Dundalk in July 1973.

Although also now converted for OMO operation, there were still individual differences between the 33 Regal IVs and AU275 which was new to Dundalk Depot as a 45 seat service bus. Outstationed at Oldcastle when CIE took over it has arrived into Dublin at 12.00 from Cavan where it was then based. It too became a school bus in 1967, being withdrawn in January 1970. Others had differing seating capacities when new and these even varied over the years. AU331-4 entered service as coaches with distinguishing V shaped flashes on the front and also cream rear wheel flashes. While 331-3 had 38 seats, 334 was fitted with 40 coach seats. However, all of 331-46 had loudspeakers when new, and every GNR vehicle had heaters, the emphasis always being on comfort.

Even after entering service with CIE in 1958, twelve of these front line vehicles (AU260-6/331/4/42-4) were converted to full luxury coach configuration in the summer of 1959 with 34 seats, and painted in the primrose and lavender livery which they kept for up to four seasons to cover an acute shortage of tour coaches. Parked beside AU267 at Dundalk Bus Station in October 1964 are AU343 from Drogheda Depot awaiting to return at 1.00 and AU334 going to Newry. AU343 actually had 40 dual purpose seats when new at Drogheda and was withdrawn as a school bus in 1992. AU334 however, delivered as a coach, entered service on the Newry run, and it survived as a school bus until October 1973.

Although the last Gardner (G402) entered service only two years before the first Regal IV (AU260) the first of 96 Gardners left the GNR works in March 1937 with production continuing until 1942 and resuming in 1947. Fifty five of these unique machines passed to CIE. While all had chassis assembled at Dundalk incorporating Gardner 5LW engines and Leyland gear boxes, the bodies fitted pre-war were all timber-framed and constructed there. However, the next batch of bodies on G361-84 had Metal Sections framing, panelled by Harkness Coachworks in Belfast with the final assembly being carried out at Dundalk. These bodies subsequently gave problems and many required substantial rebuilding such as G376, photographed after withdrawal at Dundalk Depot in 1964. New in December 1947, it had been operating at Stranorlar when acquired by CIE and had only recently been taken out of service.

While all the GNR single decks taken over by CIE had roof luggage carriers, the C class introduced in 1965 were CIE's first provincial buses constructed without them. Designed with peaked domes as seen on C118 at Dundalk Bus Station in 1982 outshopped in cherry red with an ivory roof, these were modified in most of this class to improve heating and ventilation as they had no opening windows but forced ventilation. C229, also allocated to Dundalk Depot, was the first to be so treated in 1970, and C125 which has arrived in at 10 am from its outstation at Castleblayney shows this feature. C118 became a school bus in 1985 painted in yellow and cream, retaining its peak dome until withdrawn in September 1992, and donating it to C234 in preservation. C125 by contrast was off tax by January 1986, and recommended for scrapping in December of that year.